Literature Study Guide

Callie's Contest of Courage

Literature Focus, Vocabulary, Discussion Questions, and Activities

Jan May

New Millennium Girl Books

Literature Study Guide

for Callie's Contest of Courage—Copyright, Jan May, 2016.

Education and Language Arts

All rights reserved. No portion of this book may be copied, shared, given away, or reproduced in any manner, whatsoever.

Printed in the United States of America

First Edition

Published by New Millennium Girl Books, 2016

Contents

Chapter 1 5
    Theme, questions, Bible verse activity, vocabulary

Chapter 2 11
    Symbolism, questions, map activity, vocabulary

Chapter 3 16
    Plot, questions, scavenger hunt activity, crossword

Chapter 4 21
    Setting, questions, butterfly box activity, word search

Chapter 5 26
    Similes, discussion questions, ice cream cups activity, word search

Chapter 6 33
    Personification, puns, questions, leaf book activity, word search

Chapter 7 . . . . **44**
    Personification & similes, questions, state report, crossword

Chapter 8 . . . . **49**
    Foreshadowing, questions, fun-fair booth activity, word match

Chapter 9 . . . . **54**
    Personification, questions, fun-fair game activity, vocabulary

Chapter 10 . . . . **60**
    Characters, questions, banana-cream pie activity, crossword

Chapter 11 . . . . **65**
    Mood, questions, balloon game review activity, word match

Chapter 12 . . . . **70**
    Symbolism, questions, support our troops activities, crossword

Answer Key. **75**

About the Author. 103

Chapter 1
Team Fleming

Literature Focus

1. A theme is the main idea that runs throughout a story. In this story the theme is having courage and faith in God during difficult times. Where in chapter one does the author begin to develop this theme?

_____

_____

2. Have you ever had to do something difficult by yourself? What was it?

_____

_____

3. What story does the author use during Bible time to set up the theme of courage and faith?

_____

Discussion Questions

1. What Bible verse does Callie's dad ask her to pray over him while he is gone overseas in the Marines? _____

2. Why do you think this Psalm is important in this situation?

_____

_____

3. Do you or your family have a favorite Bible verse you pray over each other like Callie's family did? If so, what is it?
_____
_____

4. Do you have siblings who annoy you? What are the some of the things they do that bother you?
_____
_____

5. Do you think that any of those things are just ways to get your attention because they want to be with you? Why or why not?
_____
_____

6. Callie loves animals. What is your favorite animal?
_____

7. Have you ever wanted to win something so badly that you were unkind to others around you? _____ What happened?
_____
_____

Activity - With the fun, bordered paper provided, write out a family verse. Cut out your verse poster and hang it where you can see it. Memorize the verse this week or use it as a nightly prayer with your family.

Vocabulary Words - Context

Instructions: Place the correct vocabulary word or phrase in the blank space in the sentence that matches it best. Choose from the words listed below:

Word List:

horizon	super telephoto lens	sergeant
hover	Philistine	deployment
internal	coat of armor	responsible
Semper Fi	cower	
camouflage	reluctant	

1. Brad was _____ to go to the game on Tuesday night because he had to wake up early for work the next day.

2. King David and the Israelites often fought against the _____ army in the Bible.

3. A helicopter can _____ in the sky, while an airplane cannot.

4. The Knights of the Round Table wore a _____ _____ to protect them in battle.

5. The sunset is a beautiful orange and pink along the _____ this evening.

6. Katie was _____ for washing the dishes and cleaning the bathroom this week.

7. The teen camp summer team went on a _____ to Haiti in June to help rebuild the city.

8. Chloe would _____ every time she went near a snake or a spider.

9. One the camping trip Mika used her _____ _____ to snag a great shot of a mother bird and her babies in a willow tree near the pond.

10. The _____ sent a command to his troops to move forward into enemy territory.

11. The change that Lilly felt was something _____, something that made her come alive.

12. The troops wore leaves, mud, and twigs as _____ to keep them from being seen by the enemy.

13. The motto of the US Marine Corps is _____, which is a Latin phrase that means "always faithful."

Chapter 2
For Daddy

Literature Focus

1. Symbolism in literature is when an author uses an object to help the reader understand something else. In this story the author uses a lion, a bear, and the giant, Goliath, to symbolize difficulties in Callie's life. What things happen in Callie's life that she thinks are like a lion, a bear, and Goliath?

Lion: _____

Bear: _____

Goliath: _____

Symbolism is also used when Callie looks out the window during a storm.

2. What does the American flag flapping in the wind symbolize?

_____

_____

Discussion Questions

1. What does Callie have to give up?

_____

2. What is her attitude about it at first?

_____

3. Have you ever had to give up something like Callie did? What helped you overcome the disappointment?
_____
_____

4. What helps Callie get over her disappointment?
_____
_____

5. Callie thinks about two tests she has overcome in the past. What are they?
_____
_____

Activity - Make a Map of Callie's Travels

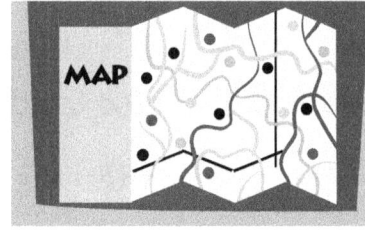

Track Callie as she travels through the next several chapters. Draw a dotted line ----- on the map to indicate the route they travel. Draw a star in the places where the family stops. Also draw and label:

    Sierra Nevada (mountains)   Pacific and Atlantic Oceans

    Rocky Mountains   Colorado Springs

    Mississippi River   bear country

    Great Salt Lake   corn fields of Iowa

    The five Great Lakes: Sweetwater, Illinois

    (Superior, Erie, Michigan, Huron, Ontario)

Vocabulary Words

Instructions: Write the correct vocabulary word or phrase in the blank part of the sentence that matches it best. Choose from the words listed below:

Word List:

Skype	protest	unravel
furrow	nerves are shot	engulfing
recognize	rides shotgun	enveloped
volunteer	embrace	
scholarship	balm of my soul	

1. Mom and Dad gave each other a warm _____ after being away from each other for a week.

2. The kitten will _____ the ball of yarn when she plays with it.

3. "I _____ that I may have gone the wrong way and now I'm lost," said Peter.

4. Instead of calling, Ashley plans to _____ with her friend Nichole, who lives in France.

5. Abi will _____ to bring cookies and ice cream to the church picnic.

6. "Writing music and poetry is a _____," said Jenna.

7. Kalen's _____ from all the stress at school and work.

8. Every time we get in the car my little dog Jackson _____ while I drive.

9. Andy won a _____ to attend Harvard University this fall.

10. Grandma _____ the newborn baby with her loving arms.

11. The town signed a petition to _____ the new mall being built over the beautiful forest.

12. The waves were _____ the surfer, who fell off his surfboard far from shore.

13. The troops dug a _____ to hide in during the dusk and dawn hours.

Chapter 3
Into Bear Country

Literature Focus

A plot is like a road map, with important stops marked along the way. It moves the story along from beginning to end, with some fun twists along the way.

1. Do you remember what the book's theme is? _____
How are the plot elements in this chapter important to developing this theme?

_____

_____

2. There are usually one or more dramatic questions raised in the reader's mind as she reads the story. These questions MUST be answered by the end of the story. After reading the first three chapters, write what you think is the first and greatest dramatic question so far:

_____

_____

3. Several other, less-dramatic questions are also raised along the way.. Name two of them.

_____

_____

_____

Discussion Questions

1. What does Mom want Callie to do with Curt in the car?
_____

2. Does your family ever play car games when they travel? _____

If so, which ones? _____

3. Why is Colorado called *bear country*?
_____
_____

4. What does Callie do to save Mom?
_____
_____

5. Callie feels confident she can chase the bear away because black bears are not aggressive. What does "not aggressive" mean?
_____
_____

6. Have you ever found yourself in a dangerous situation? Write about it. What did you do? How did it end?
_____
_____

Activity – Create a Travel Scavenger Hunt Game!

Have each person in class make a list of things they might see on a car ride. Make 8 to 10 of them *easy*, such as a blue car, traffic light, or a fast food restaurant. Then make 8 to 10 difficult items, such as a driver wearing a hat, a license plate from a far-away state, or Volkswagen Beetle. See who can find *all* of the items on the list first. Happy hunting!

Find These Easy Items

1. _____
2. _____
3. _____
4. _____
5. _____
6. _____
7. _____
8. _____
9. _____
10. _____

Find These Hard Items

1. _____
2. _____
3. _____
4. _____
5. _____
6. _____
7. _____
8. _____
9. _____
10. _____

Vocabulary Words - Crossword Puzzle

Instructions: Read the clues listed below. Words will be written either across the puzzle or down the puzzle. Write the word in the spaces listed.

Word List

mimic	envision	scenic route
bewildered	never	species
albino	symbiotic	foothill
adjusted	internship	frantically
publish	console	

Words Across:

3. to have adapted oneself to conditions

7. a paid or unpaid position with emphasis on training rather than employment; usually temporary

9. a cooperative relationship

11. to be confused, especially when having a great many things to worry about

12. to imitate someone or their actions or words

13. a beautiful course one can sometimes travel (use a dash (-) in the puzzle to separate the two words)

Words Down:

1. a hill at the foot of higher hills or mountains

2. to comfort (someone) during a time of grief or disappointment

4. to imagine as a future possibility; to visualize

5. anxiously, worriedly, or wildly excited

6. not ever; at no time

8. the preparation and issuing of a book, journal, piece of music, or other work for public sale

9. one of the basic units of biological classification and rank

10. an organism deficient (lacking) in coloring matter (pigment)

Chapter 4
Twins of Mischief

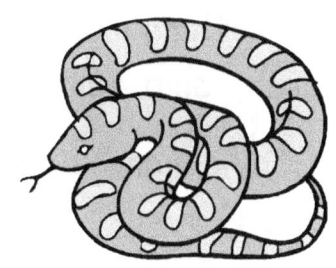

Literature Focus

The setting of a book is "where" and "when" the story takes place. In this chapter the setting is Colorado Springs, Colorado. The time is summer.

A *sensory* setting is when an author uses all five senses to describe the setting to the readers. This way the reader does not just read the story but also experiences it through their senses.

The five senses are sight, sound, smell, taste, and touch. In the sentences below, write which of the five senses the author uses to describe the setting in the story.

1. There were cozy blue and white braided rugs and white wicker furniture. _____

2. Curt and Tory bounded through the grass together chasing crickets. "I caught one," giggled Curt. "It tickles my hand." _____

3. Callie thought the puffy white clouds reminded her of cotton candy.
_____

4. Jesse plopped down on the soft grass and tucked his arms behind his curly head. _____

5. The crickets sang in the grass. Monarch butterflies played in the bushes, and tiny chipmunks scurried among the logs. (two senses)
_____   _____

6. "Nothing like ice-cold, pink lemonade and sugar cookies on the front porch," said Aunt Maddie, carrying a tray. _____

7. Callie marveled that a smelly old cow could give such sweet milk for ice cream. _____

8. Callie dipped her foot into the edge of the water. "It's nice and cool. I want to dive in and splash around like a fish." _____

Discussion Questions

1. Why are Jack and Jesse called the twins of mischief?
_____

2. What do the twins like to do that Callie admires?
_____

3. What kind of imaginary games do you like to play? _____
_____
_____

4. Jack has a cool belt with three things on it. What are they?
_____

5. Name some animals Callie sees while she's staying at Jack and Jesse's house.
_____
_____

6. Which animal does Callie say would make a good pet?
_____

Vocabulary Words - Word Search

Instructions: Circle the nine vocabulary words in the puzzle below. (See word list that follows.) Words can be found vertically, horizontally, or diagonally. When you have finished, look up the definitions and write them next to the words. Happy searching!

```
S E M E R G E U E N T C G B B
E H A X E Z P R O S I O V D F
K B U N B B C T S T H M M M C
U V F C E Y O O Q R V P A F M
H G T E K R C W P A S E A G V
B R L F I I P P O J T T I U J
U H W O R H N P Z Y F I E S Q
C N U X D Q C G D R Y T C X M
H S M M Q T C S C T D I A P G
S U O I C S U L I O C V M P V
Y J G U O D E B E M R E I A W
K A I V H V L D I N E N R X K
Z E E H R N J N P V C A G E C
W I F A J K Z J M H R H O O S
W C M Y W X T Z Y J P B D Q H
```

*Note: There are no spaces in the word search. Number 9, "shucking corn" can be found as one long word.

23

Word List - Write out the definitions

1) CLENCH -
_____
_____

2) COMPETITIVE -
_____
_____

3) EMERGE -
_____
_____

4) GRIMACE -
_____
_____

5) LUSCIOUS -
_____
_____

6) MARVEL -
_____
_____

7) MISCHIEF -
_____
_____

8) NOTORIOUS -
_____
_____

9) SHUCKING CORN -
_____
_____

Activity-Make a Butterfly Box

- Take a large box about 12" x 18" x 18"

- Make a habitat for the butterflies by putting grass, flowers, milkweed pods, plants, sticks or rocks on the bottom.

- Use a lid from a jar or other small shallow dish and add 1 teaspoon of sugar. Fill it with water. Mix until it dissolves. Place it in the bottom of the box for the butterflies to drink.

- Slip the box inside of a clear plastic bag. Look for clear kitchen or dry-cleaner bags.

- Catch live butterflies using a net. You will need to be quiet and walk slowly up to them. Place them in a small box or plastic container with holes so they can breathe until you transplant them into the Butterfly Box. Give them water like above.

- Watch the butterflies slurp up the sugar water through the plastic. Use a magnifying glass to see their curly tongues!

- Keep for a day or two, and then release them back into the wild.

Chapter 5
Water Balloon Bombs

Literature Focus

A **simile** is a figure of speech that compares one thing to another using "like" or "as" to give a better picture of what something is like. The author uses many **similes** in this chapter. Below are nine of them.

What do the following similes mean?

1. The stars were like white sprinkles on a chocolate cake.

   _____

   _____

2. Her email was like a ghost town.

   _____

   _____

3. Callie ventured out into the cool summer morning like an eager reporter looking for a hot news tip.

   _____

   _____

4. The butterflies fanned their wings as if they were parading in the early morning light for all to see.

   _____

   _____

26

5. The kids looked like a band of starving pirates who had been out to sea too long.

_____

_____

6. Callie felt like a butterfly emerging from a chrysalis.

_____

_____

7. The twins were so startled by the loud noise that they popped up like pieces of toast in a toaster.

_____

_____

8. Water balloons pummeled the boys like bombs.

_____

_____

9. Hope in Callie's heart was growing like a weed.

_____

_____

Discussion Questions

1. Callie is tempted to do something but stops herself. What is it?
_____

2. Why is this considered unwise for a military family?
_____
_____

3. What does Callie quote that helps her stay strong? _____
What does it mean? _____

4. Why does Callie compare her life to the DNA "mush" in the butterfly chrysalis?
_____
_____

5. What does Callie remember Mrs. Peters saying in Sunday school about our lives?
_____
_____

6. The twins of mischief did something to Curt and Callie the last time they were visiting that makes Callie cautious. What was it?
_____
_____

7. What does Callie think might be a trick of the twins when they get into the tree house?
_____
_____

Activity-Callie's Yummy Ice Cream Cups

Makes eight 5-oz ice cream desserts

Supplies:

Eight 5-ounce paper cups

Eight popsicle sticks

Ingredients:

1 quart vanilla ice cream, softened but not runny

Oreo cookies, roughly chopped

6 ounces of warm, chocolate fudge topping (not hot)

6 ounces caramel topping

6 ounces mini-chocolate chips

1 cup chopped nuts

Chopped M&Ms

6 to 10 peanut butter cups, chopped

Directions: Have a variety of ingredients on hand so that each person can make their own special flavor. Then begin layering in the paper cups. Start with the nuts or other candy topping, then add a small softened scoop of ice cream followed by chocolate or caramel sauce, then cookies or candies. Repeat. Put a popsicle stick in the middle of each cup. Freeze for 2 hours or until ice cream hardens. Use a scissors to cut a slit in the top of the paper cup, then tear it off and enjoy! The twins of mischief love these with gummy worms!

Vocabulary Words - Word Search

Instructions: Circle the twelve vocabulary words in the puzzle below. (See word list that follows.) Words can be found vertically, horizontally, or diagonally. When you have finished, look up the definitions and write them next to the words. Happy searching!

```
N U F X N E I R N S E G V Y L
M O Q G L Q T U U Z V H L X E
Z P O B Z H E O G S I O M M M
R U A M A Q I B I H S S X E M
G N V K T C O T T O S T R O U
E T K W I N U B O B E T A L P
H T E P V A E Y O X R O Q Y P
B S S R T F E C G Q G W R N T
Y U I I R D Q R S Q G N O V S
S E O S E I Q U U E A A Y K L
E N C O U N T E R T R M U K C
U F K N O U Z O Y A N C Q H D
T H G I L Y K S R O Y E S U W
G G D G I T Q Y V Y P F V D Y
Q L T G F G Y E R S I B Z A A
```

*Note: There are no spaces in the word search. Number 3, "crescent moon," can be found as one long word.

30

Word List - Write out the definitions

1) AGGRESSIVE -

_____

_____

2) VENTURE -

_____

_____

3) CRESCENT MOON -

_____

_____

4) TERRITORY -

_____

_____

5) ENABLE -

_____

_____

6) ENCOUNTER -

_____

_____

7) GHOSTTOWN -
_____
_____

9) PUMMEL -
_____
_____

10) SITUATION -
_____
_____

11) SKYLIGHT -
_____
_____

12) SUSPICIOUS -
_____
_____

Chapter 6
Sweetwater

Literature Focus

1. When Callie goes into Nana's garden, what character from literature does she feel like?
_____

2. Why does she feel like this? _____
_____

Personification is a literary device used when a nonliving thing is given the qualities of a person. At the top of page 75 it says "Bitterness seized its opportunity and pounced on Callie like a hungry lion. It choked out any glimmer of forgiveness." Bitterness isn't a person, but here it is used like one to get across an idea.

Write one way you think bitterness can be like a hungry lion.

_____
_____

When Callie said she was "itching" to show Dad her new pictures and then added, "No pun intended," she was using a literary device called a *pun*. A pun is a play on words and is intended to be funny. A pun is created by using a word that has two or more meanings . . . or by using similar sounding words that have different meanings.

When Callie was "itching" to show Dad her picture, she remembered the time she had poison ivy and itched a lot. When she realized she made a pun, she said, "No pun intended." This meant she made a pun accidentally, but it was funny anyway. At the very end of the book, Curt asks if they can stop off at Jack and Jesse's house on their way home to California. Grandpa says that Callie is just *itching* to go there. He *does* mean to make a pun this time. He makes them all laugh.

Discussion Questions

1. Callie gets into poison ivy. What does her mother put on it?
_____

2. Have you ever gotten poison ivy before? _____ Tell about it.
_____
_____

3. Whom does Callie believe is playing a trick on her?
_____

4. What was the Great Chicago Fire?
_____
_____
_____

5. Why does Mickey say that Mr. Nutty could sometimes be a pest?
_____
_____

6. What does Mickey mean when he says "a leaf of three, let it be" about poison ivy?
_____

Activity - Make a Leaf Book

Cut out the boxes and staple them together. Choose the correct name for each leaf and write it on the line under the picture. Go on a nature walk and see if you can find all the leaves on the next two pages. The blank boxes are for you to draw a picture a leaf that is not shown here. Look up poison ivy and draw it in one of the boxes. Be careful not to touch it!

Vocabulary Words - Word Search

Instructions: Circle the fourteen vocabulary words in the puzzle below. (See word list that follows.) Words can be found vertically, horizontally, or diagonally. When you have finished, look up the definitions and write them next to the words. Happy searching!

```
E T N Y S Q J O Q L F P C A M
N L T N D T H T P B O T T U I Y
T Z P J I C C O E P P E M D H V
H I P E D K H A U A C M W B P I
R J L S E S S L F E C E H T O N
A T M V N T A M I I S E O X R O
L H U W W T S P O T T Q F D T S
L V A Z I V R H E L M R N C S I
E P D O Z E F R C V D W A J A O
D M N X T A N T V R O E L T T P
I Z S S Q S T L G F U T R O A U
I M A M T Z D F W F L H N I C S
X M D A C O N S C I E N C E N J
D E T N A H C N E N S F T V K G
Q E G N I P P O R D S E V A E N
S A B U N D A N T X L V D R L E
```

*Note: There are no spaces in the word search. Numbers 2, 3, 4, and 9 can be found as long words run together.

40

Word List – Write out the definitions

1) ABUNDANT -

_____

_____

2) MID-WESTERN STATES -

_____

_____

3) PAWN SHOP -

_____

_____

4) POISON IVY -

_____

_____

5) POPULATION -

_____

_____

6) SMOLDERING -

_____

_____

7) ARTIFACTS -

_____

_____

8) CATASTROPHIC -

_____

_____

9) CHURCH STEEPLE -

_____

_____

10) CONSCIENCE -

_____

_____

11) EAVESDROPPING -

_____

_____

12) ENCHANTED -

_____

_____

13) ENTHRALLED -

_____

_____

14) MASTERPIECE -

_____

_____

Chapter 7

Hope

Literature Focus

1. Similes have been mentioned before. On page 78 it says, "Stubbornness set in like concrete, and angry clouds settled over Callie." How do these two similes give a good word picture of how she is feeling?

_____

_____

2. Personification is a literary device (or tool) that authors use to show different feelings and moods. When Callie sees Mickey's house, she thinks the house looks sad. Houses can't really look sad. They don't have emotions like people do, but using personification helps the reader understand the mood of the scene in the story.

Why does Callie think the house looks sad? _____

_____

_____

3. Mickey uses a saying about sheep. "The grass is always greener on the other side." What does this saying mean?

_____

4. Why do you think this saying might be true? _____

_____

_____

_____

Discussion Questions

1. How does God speak to Callie? _____
_____
_____

2. How does God speak to us? _____
_____
_____

3. When Callie forgives Mickey, she feels as if a burden has rolled away from her shoulders. Why do you think she feels this way?
_____
_____
_____

4. What do you think is the significance of the sheep's name "Hope"?
_____
_____
_____

Activity - Write a State Report

Choose your state (or another) and write a brief report using the outline on the next page. On a separate sheet of paper, draw a map of the state and add geographical features. Include pictures of crops that are grown there and other means of commerce. Share it with the group.

USA STATE REPORT

Name of state: _____

Meaning of the name: _____

State bird: _____

Other wildlife: _____
_____

Where is this state located in the USA? north, south, east, west, etc.
_____

Climate: _____

Major rivers: _____

Other bodies of water: _____

What is the state's terrain? (flat, mountainous, hilly?): _____
_____
_____

Industry and commerce: _____
_____
_____

Presidents who were born here: _____
_____

Famous people who live here: _____
_____

45

Vocabulary Words - Crossword Puzzle

Instructions: Read the clues listed below. Words will be written either across or down the puzzle in the squares below. There is a vocabulary word listed for each space in the puzzle.

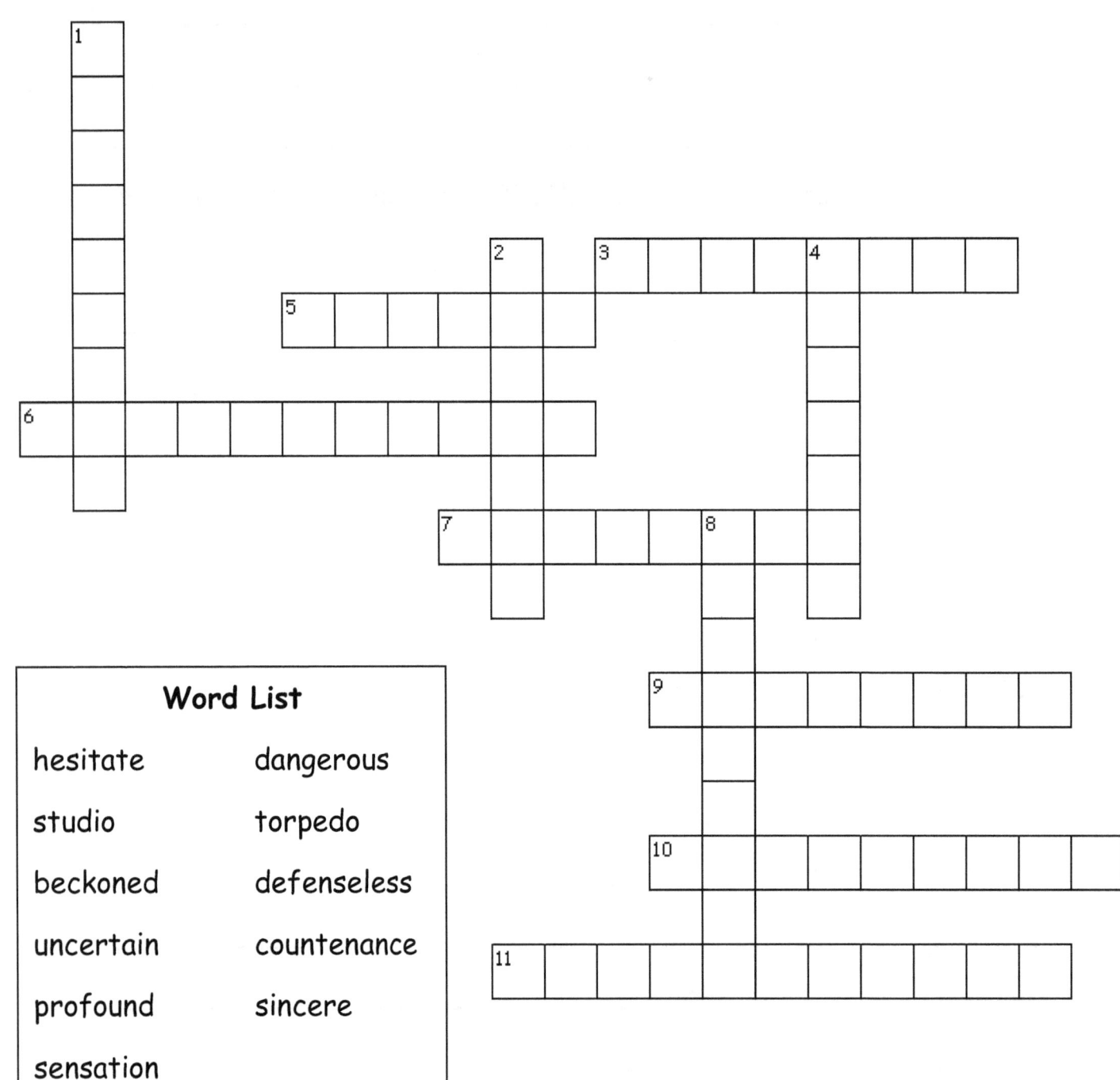

Word List

- hesitate
- studio
- beckoned
- uncertain
- profound
- sensation
- dangerous
- torpedo
- defenseless
- countenance
- sincere

Words Across:

3. to stop or pause because of uncertainty

5. a room where an artist, photographer, sculptor, etc., works

6. an expression on the face showing emotions

7. very deeply felt; immense; huge

9. to call or signal to a person, usually by a wave or a nod

10. not safe; involving danger

11. without protection; vulnerable

Words Down

1. a cause or feeling of excitement

2. genuine; real; trustworthy

4. a thin, self-propelled submarine weapon

8. not sure; not certain

Chapter 8
Prayer Meeting

Literature Focus

1. When Callie says the reason Mickey wore the hat was that it was *meant to be*, she is using something called *foreshadowing*. The author is giving the reader a clue that something important is going to happen. What does Callie foreshadow in this chapter?

_____

_____

2. The author uses symbolism again on page 95. What conclusion(s) does Callie come to after realizing she is becoming courageous?

_____

_____

_____

_____

3. Think back to a time when you felt like you had to face a type of "lion" or "bear" situation (big and scary). Describe it. How did you overcome your fear? _____

_____

_____

_____

_____

Discussion Questions

1. Nana says that Callie's dad is underneath the Lord's wings. What does this mean?

_____

_____

2. Nana also says that faith knows something is true deep down inside, even if you can't see it with your eyes. That's when you have to use your faith muscles. Think of a time in your life when you or someone around you had to use faith muscles for something. Describe the event.

_____

_____

_____

3. Callie says she will have sweet dreams tonight now that her fight with Mickey was over. Why does she say this?

_____

_____

4. What is the best way to handle a fight and not lose sleep?

_____

_____

5. Which picture does Callie end up choosing? Why does she choose this one?

_____

_____

_____

6. From reading the chapter, what do you think a "prayer vigil" is? Have you ever attended a prayer vigil? _____ If "yes," What was it like?

_____

_____

7. Pastor Nelson says that God's eyes roam to and fro around the earth looking for those whose hearts are wholly His, to support them. What does he mean?

_____

_____

8. When Pastor Nelson is speaking and quoting passages of the Bible, something happens in Callie's heart. What is it?

_____

_____

_____

Activity - Draw a Fun-Fair Booth

If you created a funfair booth what would it look like? Partner with another person and brainstorm ideas. Think of a catchy name for your booth using alliteration An alliteration uses the same beginning sound for each word: Pattie's Pink Penny Toss; Frank's Fantastic Fish Tank. Then draw a picture of your booth and decorate it with sequins, stickers, etc. to present to the group.

Vocabulary Words - Match the definitions

Instructions: Below is a list of definitions and words. Match the correct word that goes with its definition by writing the letter in the blank (see word list below).

Definition List:

1) _____ a girl or woman who milks cows or does other work in a dairy

2) _____ a military stronghold, especially a strongly fortified place

3) _____ a fatal, epidemic disease

4) _____ to stare openly and stupidly

5) _____ a shelter or protection from danger or distress

6) _____ to taste (good food or drink) and enjoy it completely

7) _____ name for a trap; and a name for a professional bird trapper

8) _____ full of danger or risk

9) _____ a sound of liquid moving around

10) _____ a piece of armor held by a handle or worn on the forearm that is used defensively to protect someone

11) _____ used to express exhilaration, especially when leaping from a great height or moving at a high-speed; also the name of a Bedonkohe Apache leader

12) _____ one of the slender posts used to support the handrail of a staircase

13) _____ a tall clock standing directly on the floor

Word List:

A) sloshing

B) banister

C) milkmaid

D) Geronimo

E) grandfather clock

F) perilous

G) pestilence

H) fortress

I) snare of the fowler

J) refuge

K) shield and buckler

L) savor

M) gawk

Chapter 9
Fun Fair

Literature Focus

In this chapter the author uses personification in this sentence: "Callie tried to suppress the mischievous thoughts crawling inside her brain." Thoughts can't really crawl inside Callie's brain, can they? But the use of this literary device spices up her feelings.

Personification is used two other times in this chapter. Find them on the pages listed below and write them down:

1. Page 105: _____

_____

2. Page 108: _____

_____

Discussion Questions

Callie can't sleep the night before the fun fair because she keeps thinking about what Mickey and Curt have. She decides to get out of bed, sneak down to their room, and listen at the door to see if she can hear anything.

1. Have you ever had a secret project that you wanted to wait and unveil when it was all finished? What was it? _____

_____

_____

2. Name two nice things Callie does for her mom before she leaves the fun fair.

_____

_____

3. Sometimes doing special things for people who feel sad is nice. Think of a time when you did something special for someone who was sad.

_____

_____

_____

Make a list of some nice things you can do for people in your life right now. The Bible says that even if you give a cup of cold water to a little one, you give it to Him.

_____

_____

_____

4. Mickey says he feels like a caterpillar when Callie talks about DNA mush. What does he mean by this?

_____

_____

_____

5. Mickey said," Mrs. Berg always says love covers a multitude of sins or something like that." What does Mrs. Berg mean?

_____

_____

6. At the end of chapter 9, Callie says she almost missed it, that God had a bigger plan than she knew about coming to Sweetwater, and that plan had to do with Mickey O'Reilly. What does Callie mean?

_____

_____

_____

7. Callie states, "How could I ever have been so wrong about Mickey?" She judged him right away. Think of a time when you judged someone at first glance and that person turned out to be someone completely different. Share on the lines below.

_____

_____

_____

_____

This saying holds true: *Never judge a book by its cover.* We should always give people a chance, even if they seem different from us.

Activity - Make a Fun Fair Game!

This is a great way to have fun and help the environment at the same time. Purchase several bags of small plastic balls in multi-colors at a dollar store. For several weeks, save up plastic recycled materials (such as lettuce or fruit containers). Wash and dry them, then start to create!

Game #1 Cut off the lids of 25 berry containers. Tape them together with clear packaging tape to form a square and create a candy-toss game. Place a piece of candy in each one. Have the players stand behind a line and toss their balls into the grid of containers. Whichever one their ball lands in, they get to keep that piece of candy!

Game #2 Use enough large lettuce containers for each player. Place 8-10 small plastic balls of the same color in each player's container. Set a timer. Each player must run around tossing their colored balls into everyone else's containers. If a balls fall on the ground, that ball is out of play. The player with the most balls in other players' containers when the buzzer rings wins a prize!

Vocabulary Words - Context

Instructions: Place the correct vocabulary word or phrase in the blank space in the sentence that matches it best. Choose from the words listed below:

Word List

Boy Scout oath	investigate	metamorphosis
amble	illustration	rearrange
festivities	gold-gilded	purchase
pine over	amazement	DNA
slather	structure	

1. Agent Rogers decided to _____ the crime scene for himself.

2. Spring is a great time to _____ the furniture for a fresh, new look in the living room.

3. Grace was excited to go to the fair and enjoy the _____.

4. When Chris saw the delicious raspberry jam, he wanted to _____ it all over his peanut butter sandwich.

5. Sara went to the Apple store to _____ a new iPhone.

6. Everyone watched their televisions in _____ when Neil Armstrong walked on the moon.

7. The _____ was originally formed in 1908, a promise of duty to God, to the king, and a promise to help others at any cost.

8. We like to _____ along the beach during the cool of the night.

9. "I would like to create an _____ for each chapter of your book, with lots of color," said Giavanna.

10. A caterpillar goes through a stage of _____ in his cocoon before he becomes a butterfly.

11. Walter, a biochemist found _____ on some of the evidence from Agent Rogers crime scene.

12. The world's largest _____ is Burj Khalifa in Dubai, which stands 2,272 feet high.

13. The old Bible on Grandpa's bookshelf is _____ and very beautiful.

14. Aaron's wife will _____ _____ the idea of her husband not being able to come home for Christmas.

Chapter 10
Pie-Eating Contest

Literature Focus

1. In literature, characters grow and change throughout the story. List two examples of how Callie has grown during this story.

_____

_____

_____

2. Characters should be like real people you know. Describe Callie and Curt by listing some of their strengths and weaknesses below:

Callie's Strengths	Callie's Weaknesses
_____	_____
_____	_____
_____	_____

Curt's Strengths	Curt's Weaknesses
_____	_____
_____	_____
_____	_____
_____	_____

Characters play a big role in every story. There are "round" characters and "flat" characters. The main characters that you know a lot about and who are most important to the story are called round characters.

Characters who are only in the story a little bit and do not have a big job in the story are called flat characters. Put an R next to the name if she or he is a round character; put an F next to the name if he or she is a flat character:

Callie_____   Mrs. McTavish _____

Nana_____   Pastor Nelson_____

April_____   Curt_____

Mickey____   Grandpa Ben_____

Discussion Questions

1. During one scene in this chapter, Callie feels as if someone has just punched her in the stomach. Why does she suddenly feel this way?

_____

_____

2. Why does Mickey want to win the contest? _____

_____

_____

3. Give an example about a time when you did something special with your dad or mom, and you wanted them to be proud of you.

_____

_____

4. Callie is happy that she's made two new friends. Why is she so willing to help April take her booth down?

_____

5. Name two things you help *your* friends do.

_____

_____

6. It's raining when Callie, Mickey, and Curt head home in the back of the pickup truck. They hold the blanket over their heads together, and Curt burps the ABC's. Why does Mickey feel like he has a family again?

_____

_____

Activity – Make Nana's Banana Cream Pie

Ingredients:

- 2 large boxes instant vanilla pudding mix
- 2-3 ripe bananas, sliced
- graham cracker crust—readymade
- 4 cups milk
- 12-oz container of Cool Whip™

1. Make the vanilla pudding as directed on the box.

2. Slice the bananas and place them on the crust, touching each other on the bottom and up the sides of the crust.

3. After the pudding gels in the refrigerator, pour it over the crust.

4. Dollop the Cool Whip™ on top of the pudding and spread evenly.

5. Sprinkle with nuts or candy sprinkles if desired.

Vocabulary Words - Crossword Puzzle

Instructions: Read the clues listed below. Words will be written either across or down the puzzle. Write the word in the squares below.

Note: *No spaces are provided in the puzzle for a word phrase. The words will run together as one.*

Word List

adorn	division	peppermint oil
challenge	grand finale	plunge
commotion	landslide	tallied
contestant	participation	
disqualified	pavilion	

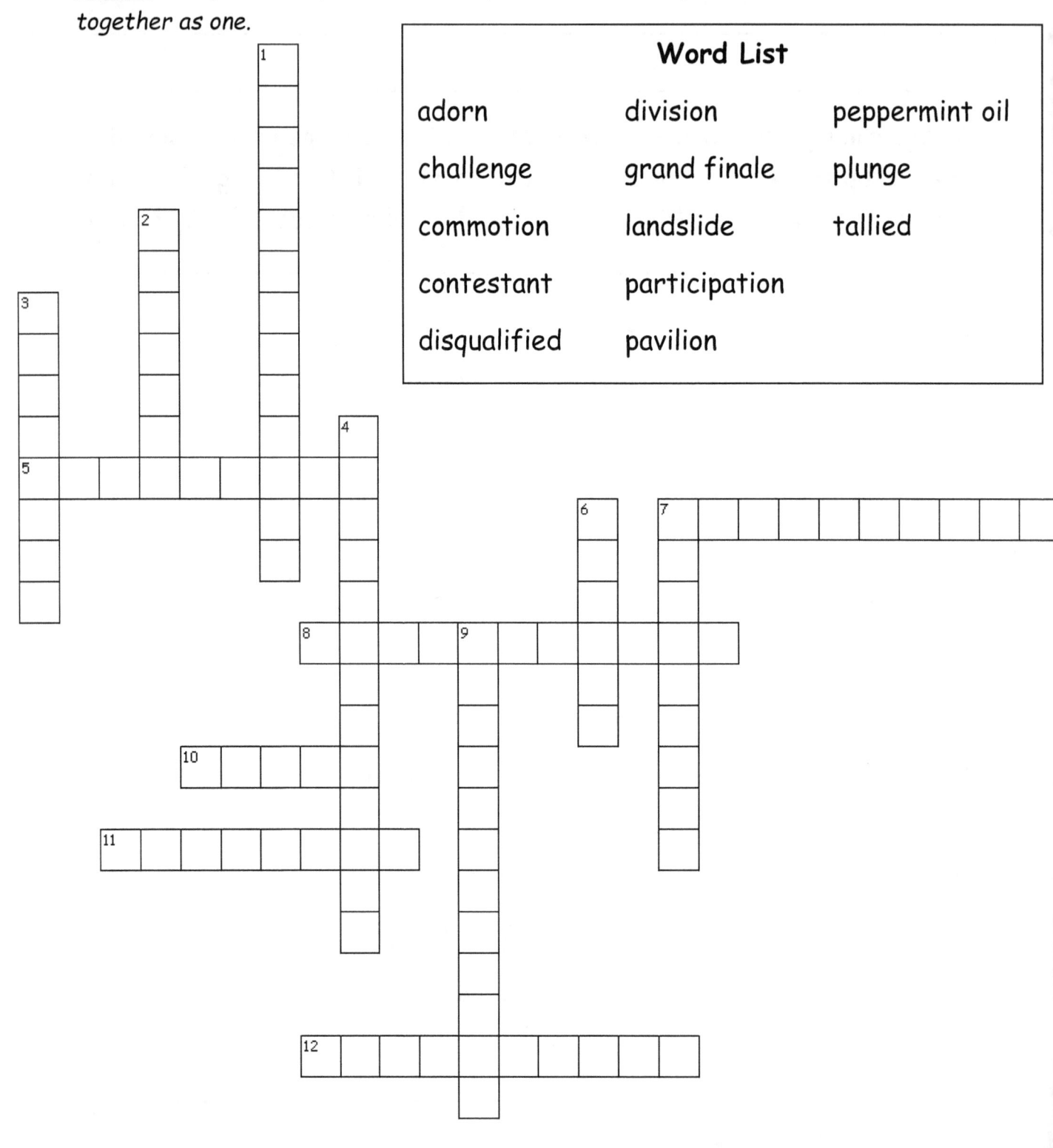

Words Across:

5. the sliding down of a mass of earth or rock from a mountain or cliff

7. a state of confused and noisy disturbance

8. a very exciting or impressive ending of a performance or show.

10. Make more beautiful or attractive

11. Something that divides, separates or a form of math where numbers divide

12. A person who takes part in a contest

Words Down

1. To take part or have a share in something in common with others

2. To keep have kept a count of

3. A building in a park or garden that usually has open sides and is used for parties, concerts, or other events

4. Oil made from peppermint leaves for flavor in food or drink, or an oil that soothes stomachs

6. To push or drive into something with force

7. To invite or dare to take part in a contest

9. To eliminate (someone) from a competition because they broke one of the rules

Chapter 11
Prayers at Midnight

Literature Focus

Sometimes in literature, the author will add weather to create a mood.

1. What mood is created by the weather in this chapter?
_____
_____

2. Does this stop Callie from praying? _____ What is her response to the storm?
_____
_____

3. When Callie finishes praying, she notices something about the storm. What does she notice?
_____
_____

4. Why do you suppose the author stops the storm just as Callie finishes praying? _____
_____

Discussion Questions

1. When Callie creeps into her mom's room after the Fun Fair, her mom is already asleep. Callie kneels down by Mom's bed and prays Psalm 91. Nana and Grandpa Ben come in and join her. When Callie sees her grandparents, she thinks they are sturdy as marble pillars. What does Callie mean when she uses this simile?

_____

_____

2. Name two miraculous things that happened to George Washington during battle in the book Callie read.

_____

_____

_____

_____

3. Think of two things you believe God can do today to protect soldiers, or to protect us when we are in danger.

_____

_____

_____

4. What was the Indian chief's response to seeing these miracles?

_____

_____

_____

5. How does Callie pray this time that is different from the way she prays at other times?

_____

_____

_____

6. Callie is surprised by the strength she had during prayer. Why?

_____

_____

_____

Activity - Play Balloon Review

Have the children bat a balloon to each other. The fifth person to bat the balloon tells their favorite part of the story. If time allows, choose two other students to act the scene out together.

Vocabulary Words - Match the Definitions

Instructions: Below and on the next page is a list of definitions and words. Match the correct word that goes with its definition by writing the alphabetical letter in the blank that it matches.

Word List:

A) emblem

B) marksman

C) mounted British officer

D) sharpshooter

E) seldom

F) realization

G) shielding

H) Great Spirit

I) probability

J) leveling

K) council

L) founder

M) empire

N) homage

O) particular

P) commander-in-chief

Definition List:

1) _____ one who founds or establishes

2) _____ making or becoming horizontal, flat, or even

3) _____ a group of people meeting to talk about important matters and to give advice

4) _____ not often

5) _____ the name the American Indians gave to God, who protected General George Washington

6) _____ special honor or respect shown publicly

7) _____ a person skilled in shooting at a mark or target

8) _____ a major political unit with a large territory or a number of territories or peoples under one ruler with total authority

9) _____ a head of state or officer in supreme command of a country's armed forces

10) _____ symbolic object used as an identifying mark

11) _____ an officer of the British army who patrols on horseback

12) _____ one skilled in shooting: a good marksman

13) _____ to be aware of

14) _____ the likelihood of something happening or being the case

15) _____ to cover or screen with or as if with a shield

16) _____ very unusual; hard to please

Chapter 12
It Ain't for Babies

Literature Focus

1. The author uses a weather simile to signify something is happening in Mickey's heart. What is it? _____

_____

_____

2. The author uses the name of the lamb, Hope, to symbolize what two things?

_____

_____

_____

_____

Discussion Questions

1. Faith and courage just come over Callie and start gushing out. Where do these qualities come from?

_____

2. Mickey asks Callie if she thinks God talks to people. What is her answer?

_____

_____

3. What are some other ways God talks to people? _____

_____

_____

4. Callie felt all grown up when she shared her faith with Mickey and how he might ask Jesus to come into his heart and take away the sin. Write down as much as you can remember of these steps.

_____

_____

_____

_____

_____

_____

5. After Mickey prays and asks God to forgive him and come into his heart, how does he feel?

_____

6. Why does it feel like a big truck has rolled off Mickey's chest?

_____

7. When Callie Skypes Dad, she confesses that she broke the camera and is ready to receive any punishment. What is Dad's response?

_____

_____

8. Callie says that she has learned something. What is it?

_____

_____

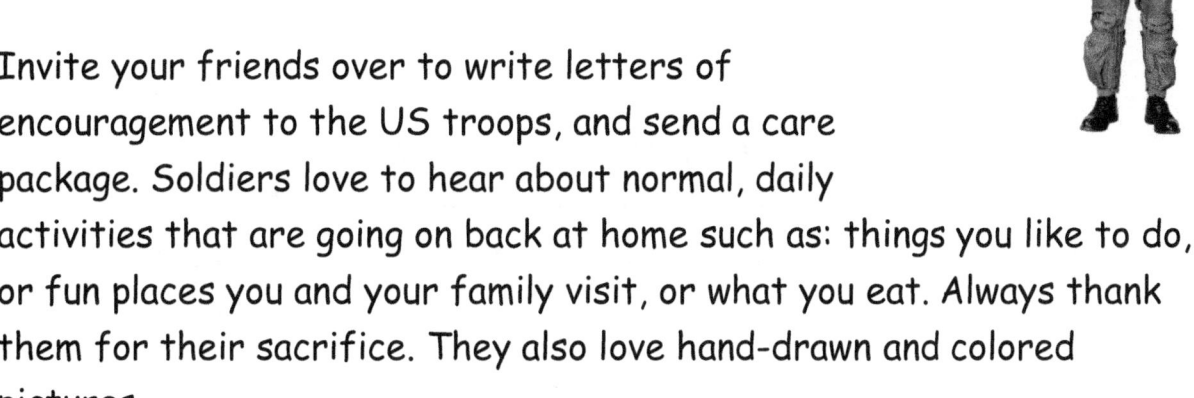

Activity – Host a "Support Our Troops" Party!

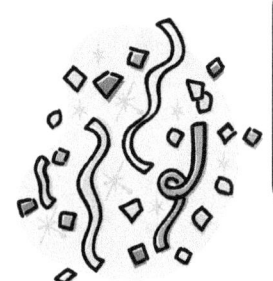

Invite your friends over to write letters of encouragement to the US troops, and send a care package. Soldiers love to hear about normal, daily activities that are going on back at home such as: things you like to do, or fun places you and your family visit, or what you eat. Always thank them for their sacrifice. They also love hand-drawn and colored pictures.

Send a Care Package to a Soldier

Have each person bring several items to include in the Solider Care Package to send it overseas. Send baked or packaged cookies, nuts, or gum. If sending it to a warm climate, don't send chocolate. Holidays are a great time to send decorations too! Always send the care packages 4-6 weeks ahead of time. A complete list of things a solider can receive, and websites to find addresses, are in the back of the book *Callie's Contest of Courage*. Include all of the letters your group writes in the package. Use a military flat rate box from the post office to fill. They are inexpensive to send. This is always the highlight in a soldier's day!

Vocabulary Words - Crossword Puzzle

Instructions: Read the clues listed below. Words will be written either across or down the puzzle. Write the word in the spaces below. There is a vocabulary word listed for each space in the puzzle.

Note: A dash (-) is between phrases to provide a space in the puzzle. Count this as one space in the puzzle.

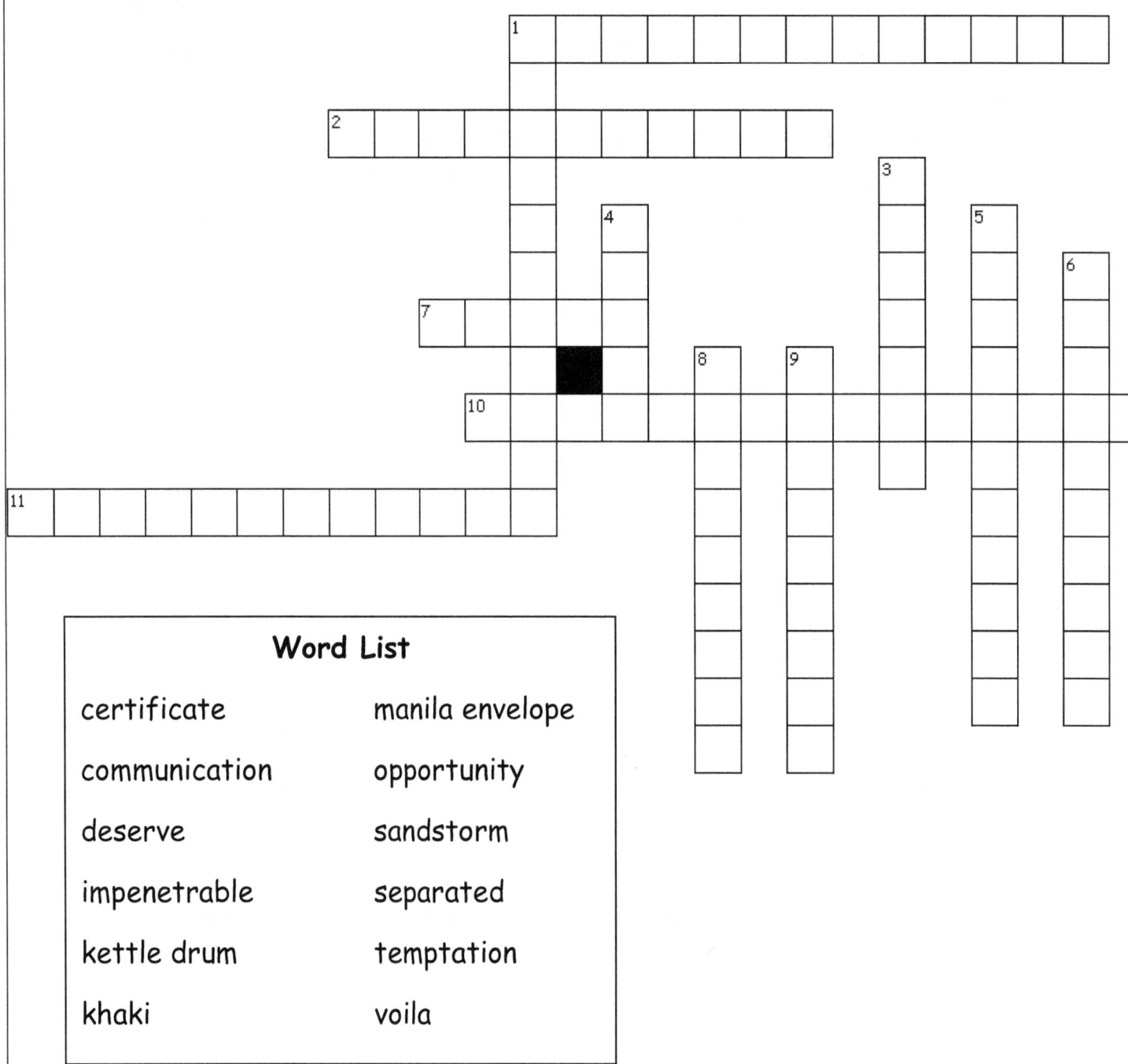

Word List

certificate	manila envelope
communication	opportunity
deserve	sandstorm
impenetrable	separated
kettle drum	temptation
khaki	voila

Words *Across:*

1. An act or instance of transmitting information

2. A favorable combination of circumstances, time, and place

7. A French exclamation meaning "there it is; there you are"

10. An envelope designed for transporting documents

11. Impossible to get through or into

Words *Down:*

1. A document that is proof of some fact

3. To be worthy of

4. A light yellowish brown color

5. A large drum shaped like a bowl, with a membrane adjustable for tension (and so pitch) stretched across.

6. The state of being tempted especially to evil

8. A storm of wind (as in a desert) that drives clouds of sand

9. To become divided or detached: come apart

Teacher's Answer Key-Literature Study Guide to Callie's Contest of Courage

Chapter 1

Literature Questions

The theme started off when Callie had to be brave when her dad deployed overseas. She had to face entering the photo contest by herself.

Discussions Questions

1. Psalm 91

2. Because it talks about how God protects people from all kinds of dangers

3. Answers will vary

4 - 7 Answers will vary

Vocabulary - Context Game

1. Reluctant

2. Philistine

3. Hover

4. Coat of Armor

5. Horizon

6. Responsible

7. Deployment

8. Cower

9. Super Telephoto Lens

10. Sergeant

11. Internal

12. Camouflage

13. Semper Fi

Definitions List:

Camouflage - the hiding or disguising of something by covering it up or changing the way it looks

Coat of armor - a unique design usually on a shield, outer garment, or a short metal coat that people wore in the Middle Ages in battle

Cower - to shrink away or crouch down (as from fear)

Deployment - to move, spread out, or place in position for some purpose like when soldiers are sent to battle

Horizon - the line where the earth or sea seems to meet the sky

Hover - to remain floating over a place or object

Internal - existing or lying within

Philistine - a member of an ancient race that lived in the coastal regions of Palestine

Reluctant - showing doubt or unwillingness

Responsible - being the one who must answer or account for something

Semper Fi - Semper fidelis is a Latin phrase that means "always faithful" or "always loyal." It is the motto of the US Marine Corps.

Sergeant - a military noncommissioned officer with any of the ranks above corporal in the army or the marines or above airman first class in the air force

Super telephoto lens – in cinematography and photography the super telephoto lens is a specific type of a long-focus lens where the object can be seen zoomed in extremely close

Chapter 2

Literature Questions

1.
- Having to give up the internship was like a lion
- Facing the bear and having courage to stand up and save her mom was like a bear
- Praying for her father who was in battle overseas was like facing Goliath

2. Her father who was not available because he was serving his country and that made her feel anxious. Dad could be in trouble because they haven't heard from him. Also Callie says after looking at the flag in the storm that her own life felt stormy.

Discussions Questions

1. The Marine Kid's Internship

2. She was angry and disappointed

3. Answers will vary

4. She realized her mom had a need greater than her own when she saw her crying and praying behind the house. She decided she would trust God and be brave like the baby sea turtles.

5. The bully at school who teased her and her broken arm

Vocabulary: Context Game

1. Embrace

2. Unravel

3. Recognize

4. Skype

5. Volunteer

6. Balm to my Soul

7. Nerves are Shot

8. Rides Shotgun

9. Scholarship

10. Enveloped

11. Protest

12. Engulfing

13. Furrow

Definitions List:

Balm to my Soul – a phrase that means to bring healing to one's heart

Embrace - to clasp in the arms, to take in: HUG

Engulfing – To sweep over, to cover completely

Enveloped - wrap up, cover, or surround completely

Furrow - a trench in the earth made by or as if by a plow

Nerves are Shot – a phrase used to say that they are under a lot of stress

Protest - a complaint, objection, or display of unwillingness or disapproval

Recognize - to be willing to admit

Rides Shotgun – a phrase means to ride in the front passenger seat in a vehicle

Scholarship - money given (as by a college or another institution) to a student to help pay for fees

Skype – A Microsoft video (picture and sound) service and instant messaging client. The name was derived from "sky" and "peer".

Unravel - to separate the threads of

Volunteer – someone who gives their services freely

Chapter 3

Literature Questions

1. Answers may vary

2. Will Callie win the photo contest?

3. How will Callie grow in Courage? Is Dad safe? Will she like Illinois?

Discussions Question

1. Play car games

2. Answers will vary

3. Because an estimated 12,000 bears live there in the wild

4. She scared the bear away from the port-a-potty

5. Black bears are one of the bear species that are not ready to attack - *wild animals are unpredictable, you should never try this!

6. Answers will vary

Vocabulary – Crossword Puzzle:

Across

3. Adjusted

7. Internship

9. Symbiotic

11. Bewildered

12. Mimic

13. Scenic Rout *(a dash is between words to provide a space in the puzzle)*

Down

1. Foothill

2. Console

4. Envision

5. Frantically

6. Never

8. Publish

9. Species

10. Albino

Definitions List:

Adjusted - to adapt oneself to conditions

Albino - an organism deficient in coloring matter

Bewildered - to confuse especially with a great many things to worry about

Console - comfort (someone) at a time of grief or disappointment

Envision - imagine as a future possibility; visualize

Foothills - a hill at the foot of higher hills or mountains

Frantically - Anxiously, Worriedly, Wildly excited

Internship – paid or unpaid temporary position with emphasis on training rather than employment

Mimic – to imitate someone or their actions or words

Never - not ever: at no time

Publish - the preparation and issuing of a book, journal, piece of music, or other work for public sale

Scenic Route – a route that is beautiful

Species - is one of the basic units of biological classification and rank

Symbiotic - a cooperative relationship

Chapter 4

Literature Questions

1. Sight

2. Touch

3. Sight

4. Touch

5. Sound and sight

6. Taste

7. Smell

8. Touch

Discussions Question

1. Because they were always playing pranks on everyone

2. They like to play imaginary games like Pirates

3. Answers will vary

4. Binoculars, a pocketknife, and an eye patch

5. Garter snake, dog named Tory, eagle, Dori the cow, crickets

6. Garter snake

Vocabulary Words - Word Search

```
S E M E R G E U E N T C G B B
E H A X E Z P R O S I O V D F
K B U N B B C T S T H M M M C
U V F C E Y O O Q R V P A F M
H G T E K R C W P A S E A G V
B R L F I I P P O J T T I U J
U H W O R H N P Z Y F I E S Q
C N U X D Q C G D R Y T C X M
H S M M Q T C S C T D I A P G
S U O I C S U L I O C V M P V
Y J G U O D E B E M R E I A W
K A I V H V L D I N E N R X K
Z E E H R N J N P V C A G E C
W I F A J K Z J M H R H O O S
W C M Y W X T Z Y J P B D Q H
```

Definitions List:

Clench - to set or close tightly

Competitive – the character of wanting to compete against ones self or others

Emerge - to become known or apparent

Grimace - a twisting of the face or features

Luscious - having a delicious taste or smell

Marvel – to be filled with wonder and amazement

Mischief - playful misbehavior or troublemaking, especially in children

Notorious - famous or well known

Shucking Corn – taking the husk (green leaves) off yellow ears of corn

Chapter 5

Literature Questions

Answers will vary

Discussions Questions

1. Checking the news on her laptop.

2. If there was fighting near where her father was stationed it might make her worry.

3. Semper fi, it's the United States Marine's motto. It means *Always Faithful*

4. That our lives may look a little messy and out of control but God is always working even when we don't see it.

5. Because her dad was gone and not able to help her with the contest and he was not keeping in touch with their family. She was worried about his safety.

6. They put shaving cream in their sleeping bags, jelly in her slippers, and spiders in her bed

7. She thought they might have put cayenne pepper or a mouse into the pie

Vocabulary Words - Word Search

```
N U F X N E I R N S E G V Y L
M O Q G L Q T U U Z V H L X E
Z P O B Z H E O G S I O M M M
R U A M A Q I B I H S S X E M
G N V K T C O T T O S T R O U
E T K W I N U B O B E T A L P
H T E P V A E Y O X R O Q Y P
B S S R T F E C G Q G W R N T
Y U I I R D Q R S Q G N O V S
S E O S E I Q U U E A A Y K L
E N C O U N T E R T R M U K C
U F K N O U Z O Y A N C Q H D
T H G I L Y K S R O Y E S U W
G G D G I T Q Y V Y P F V D Y
Q L T G F G Y E R S I B Z A A
```

Definitions List:

Encounter - to come upon face-to-face

Aggressive - being forceful in getting things done

Territory - an assigned area for a specific people or purpose

Ghost town – a city or place that doesn't have anyone or very little people that live there

Venture - to go ahead in spite of danger

Skylight - a window or group of windows in a roof or ceiling

Crescent Moon – when the moon is curved shaped in the sky

Pummel – to beat or pound

Situation - a circumstance in which one finds oneself

Enable - to make able

Suspicious - likely to suspect or distrust

Chapter 6

Literature Questions

1. Alice in Wonderland

2. The flowers were so abundant and beautiful that it was like being in a fairyland. The tall flowers bowed in the breeze as if to say hello. She bowed back and giggled. She wanted to find the white rabbit.

Discussions Questions

1. Pink calamine lotion.

2. Answers will vary

3. Yes the twins of mischief

4. A firestorm that burned for nearly two days in 1871. Roughly 3.3 square miles (9 km2) of the city of Chicago, Illinois was destroyed because the buildings were made of wood. A popular myth is to have said that it was started by Mrs. O'Leary's cow that kicked over a lantern in her barn.

5. Because if you continue to feed a wild animal he will come back for more all the time. *Squirrels are known to be a pest by eating everything out of the birdfeeder or building a nests in attics.*

6. Poison ivy is known for having three leaflets. The rhyme reminds people to beware of plants with three leaflets.

Vocabulary Words - Word Search

```
E T N Y S Q J O Q L F P C A C M
N L T N D T H T P B O T T U I Y
T Z P J I C C O E P P E M D H V
H I P E D K H A U A C M W B P I
R J L S E S S L F E C E H T O N
A T M V N T A M I I S E O X R O
L H U W W T S P O T T Q F D T S
L V A Z I V R H E L M R N C S I
E P D O Z E F R C V D W A J A O
D M N X T A N T V R O E L T T P
I Z S S Q S T L G F U T R O A U
I M A M T Z D F W F L H N I C S
X M D A C O N S C I E N C E N J
  D E T N A H C N E N S F T V K G
  Q E G N I P P O R D S E V A E N
  S A B U N D A N T X L V D R L E
```

Definitions List:

Mid Western states – A group of the United States that are in the middle, have been defined by the federal government: Illinois, Indiana, Iowa, Kansas, Michigan, Minnesota, Missouri, Nebraska, North Dakota, Ohio, South Dakota, and Wisconsin. It includes much of the Great Plains, the region of the Great Lakes, and the upper Mississippi River valley.

Poison Ivy - a North American climbing plant of the cashew family that secretes an irritant oil from its leaves, which can cause itchy or stinging on the skin

Artifacts - an object made by a human being, typically an item of cultural or historical interest

Population - the whole number of people living in a country or region

Church Steeple - a tower structure that has a belfry, a section for a lantern and on the top a spire on a church building

Masterpiece - a work done with great skill

Enthralled - captured or fascinated

Abundant - existing or available in large quantities; plentiful

Enchanted - filled (someone) with great delight; charm

Catastrophic - a sudden huge disaster

Smoldering - burn slowly with smoke but no flame

Conscience - knowledge of right and wrong and a feeling one should do what is right

Eavesdropping - secretly listen to a conversation

Pawn Shop - a business where people buy and sell previously owned items.

Chapter 7

Literature Questions

1. Answers will vary

2. The flower box was empty like no one took the time to plant flowers; the garden was overgrown with weeds because there was no one to tend it. Callie thought it looked as if summers cheery feeling had abandoned it.

3. Because sheep are not content with grass in their pasture unless it is long and sweet. They will sometimes break through the fence that is protecting them to find the tall sweet grass even if their search takes them to dangerous places like

over a cliff. People too think sometimes they would be happier if they had something over on the other side of the fence in someone else's life.

4. Because everyone has problems that others don't always see. Hard work goes into everything that people have and sacrifice for those things that we don't always see.

Discussions Questions

1. Through the Bible when she picked it up and opened the passage to "forgive others as I have forgiven you". Did this soften her heart? Yes a little but then stubbornness came.

2. Through reading the Bible, listening to sermons, going to church, through worship, and that still small voice inside, our conscience.

3. Bitterness can hold us captive to its angry feelings and it makes us feel heavy with worry and anger.

4. Yes, because hope to overcome the sadness of his mother's death was bubbling up in Mickey's life.

Vocabulary Words - Crossword Puzzle

Across

3. Hesitate

5. Studio

6. Countenance

7. Profound

9. Beckoned

10. Dangerous

11. Defenseless

Down

1. Sensation

2. Sincere

4. Torpedo

8. Uncertain

Definitions List:

Beckoned - to call or signal to a person usually by a wave or nod

Countenance - An expression on the face showing emotions

Dangerous – Not safe, involving danger

Defenseless – with our protection, vulnerable

Hesitate - to stop or pause because of uncertainty

Profound- very deeply felt, immense, huge

Sensation - a cause or feeling of such excitement

Sincere – genuine, real, trustworthy

Studio - a room where an artist, photographer, sculptor, etc., works

Torpedo - a thin self-propelled submarine weapon

Uncertain - not sure

Chapter 8

Literature Questions

1. Yes, the picture won the contest.

2. That she had overcome *a kind of* lion which was scary and big situation in the in leaving her home and losing the Marine kids internship. She had overcome the fear and danger of facing a real bear. Now she thought that this challenge of praying and believe for her daddy safety was like the giant Goliath.

3. Answers will vary

Discussions Questions

1. Just as a bird will open its wings for its young to hide underneath when bad weather or predators come so the Lord keeps us safe under his protection when we are in danger.

2. Answers will vary

3. Sometimes our conscience wrestles with us even in the middle of the night when we know we should do something that we're not doing.

4. To forgive quickly!

5. The book says it stuck out like a neon sign. Sometimes God speaks to us by letting something stick out to us like a neon sign.

 It means that it jumps out to us and catches our attention.

6. A special meeting where people gather to pray for a special cause. Christians have them because they believe that God listens to the requests of his people that there is power in unity when we pray something together. In the Bible it says if you ask anything together in my name I will do it: *"Again I say[c] to you that if two of you agree on earth concerning anything that they ask, it will be done for them by My Father in heaven. (Matthew 18:19)*

7. It means that God searches the earth back and forth to find those who have hearts that are totally dedicated to him to support them and help them.

8. The words were sinking into her soul and producing a bumper crop of hope. A bumper crop is when a farmer's crop produces an overabundance.

Vocabulary Words - Match the Definitions

1. C

2. H

3. G

4. M

5. J

6. L

7. I

8. F

9. A

10. K

11. D

12. B

13. E

Definitions List:

Banister - one of the slender posts used to support the handrail of a staircase

Fortress - a military stronghold, especially a strongly fortified place

Gawk – to stare openly and stupidly

Geronimo - used to express exhilaration, especially when leaping from a great height or moving at a high speed. Geronimo was also a Bedonkohe Apache leader.

Grandfather clock - a tall clock standing directly on the floor

Milkmaid - a girl or woman who milks cows or does other work in a dairy

Perilous - full of danger or risk

Pestilence - a fatal epidemic disease

Refuge - shelter or protection from danger or distress

Savor - taste (good food or drink) and enjoy it completely

Shield and buckler - a shield is a piece of armor that is used defensively to protect someone and a buckler is a small, round shield held by a handle or worn on the forearm

Sloshing - a sound of liquid moving around

Snare of the Fowler - a snare is a trap and the fowler is a professional bird trapper

Chapter 9

Literature Questions

1. Page 103, 5th paragraph down, "A fresh morning breeze floated through the open window and tickled Callie's nose."

2. Page 108, 2nd paragraph down, "A huge food tent with tables and chairs flapped in the wind, waiting for hungry customers."

Discussions Questions

1. Answers will vary

2. She picked flowers from the garden before she left the fun fair and she bought her a special piece of rhubarb pie at the fair. Answers will vary

3. His life felt out of control since his mom died. He felt confused and all mixed up.

4. That when someone does something to hurt us and we responded in the good and loving way we are covering their sin and forgiving it.

5. That helping Mickey overcome the grief of his mother was part of God's plan for Callie's family. Mickey needed a loving family to be a part of. She also led him to Jesus which helped them to let go of his anger towards God that his mothers death.

6. Answers will vary

Vocabulary - Context Game

1. Investigate
2. Rearrange
3. Festivities
4. Slather
5. Purchase
6. Amazement
7. Boy Scouts Oath
8. Amble
9. Illustration
10. Metamorphosis
11. DNA
12. Structure
13. Gold-Guilded
14. Pine Over

Definitions List:

Amazement - great surprise or astonishment

Amble- walk or move at a slow, relaxed pace

Boy Scout's oath – a vow boy scouts take to keep the Scout Law, a promise:

Original 1908 text:

Before he becomes a scout, a boy must take the scout's oath, thus: On my honor I promise that...

1. I will do my duty to God and the King.
2. I will do my best to help others, whatever it costs me.

3. I know the scout law, and will obey it.

While taking this oath the scout will stand, holding his right hand raised level with his shoulder, palm to the front, thumb resting on the nail of the digitus minimus (little finger) and the other three fingers upright, pointing upwards: This is the scout's salute and secret sign.

DNA – "deoxyribonucleic acid", a self-replicating material present in nearly all living organisms, it is the carrier of genetic information

Festivities - the celebration of something in a joyful and exciting way

Gold – Gilded – crafted or covered with gold

Illustration - a picture or diagram that explains or decorates

Investigate - to study by close examination

Metamorphosis - an extraordinary change in appearance, character, or circumstances

Pine Over – to long for

Purchase – to gain something, a material item, by paying for it

Rearrange - to arrange again usually in a different way

Slather - spread or smear (a substance) thickly or liberally

Structure - something constructed or arranged in a definite pattern of organization

Chapter 10

Literature Questions

1. Callie is learning not to be selfish by choosing to go to Nana's with a good attitude. She learned that being angry with someone causes you to feel yucky inside and forgiveness is the better way. She is learning that God has a good plan for her life and she can trust in that.

2. Callie's Strengths   Callie's Weakness

   smart   stubborn

   loves God   fights with Curt
   brave   selfish

Curt's Strengths   Curt's Weakness

   fun-loving   annoys sister

   loves family   mischievous

Discussions Questions

1. She felt guilty that Mickey traded his art supplies for her camera especially since it wasn't his fault. She had such a tantrum about it.

2. Because it was something fun he did with his dad and gave him good memories. He wanted to win so his dad would pay attention to him and be proud of him.

3. Answers will vary

4. Friends help each other.

5. Answers will vary

6. Because Curt was felt free to be silly in his presence and Callie included him to hold up the blanket he felt like he was a part of their family.

Vocabulary Words - Crossword Puzzle

Word List:

Across:

5. Landslide

7. Commotion

8. Grand Finale *(a dash is between words to provide a space in the puzzle)*

10. Adorn

11. Division

12. Contestant

Down:

1. Participation

2. Tallied

3. Pavilion

4. Peppermint Oil *(a dash is between words to provide a space in the puzzle)*

6. Plunge

7. Challenge

9. Disqualified

Definitions List:

Adorn - make more beautiful or attractive

Challenge - to invite or dare to take part in a contest

Commotion - a state of confused and noisy disturbance

Contestant - a person who takes part in a contest

Disqualified – to eliminate (someone) from a competition because they broke one of the rules

Division - something that divides, separates

Grand Finale - a very exciting or impressive ending of a performance or show.

Landslide - the sliding down of a mass of earth or rock from a mountain or cliff

Participation - to take part or have a share in something in common with others

Pavilion - a building in a park or garden that usually has open sides and is used for parties, concerts, or other events

Peppermint Oil – oil made from peppermint leaves for flavor in food or drink, or an oil that soothes stomachs

Plunge - to push or drive into something with force

Tallied - to keep a count of

Chapter 11

Literature Questions

1. A fight and clashing mood-the thunder answered back as if to fight with her and the rain beat against the house. A tree branch broke off and beat against the house.

2. No, she was determined and with the Lord's strength fought the spiritual battle around her for her dad's safety.

3. That it has stopped. The author stopped the storm to signify that her prayers were answered.

Discussions Questions

1. That they were very strong even in times of trouble and a good support to her and her family.

2. Ten-Twelve rounds of bullets were shot at him by Native American sharpshooters and four bullets went through his coat and they did not harm him! Two horses were shot from underneath him and he grabbed a stray one and got back up and kept on fighting.

3. Answers will vary

4. He believed that Gorge Washington was protected by the Great Spirit because he was a favorite of heaven, they should leave him alone.

5. She picked up 5 imaginary stones like David did when he defeated Goliath and Marched around the room like she was in battle herself. Some Christians call this intercessory prayer.

6. She had never prayed like that before.

Vocabulary Words - Match the Definitions

1. M
2. J
3. L
4. E
5. H
6. O
7. B
8. N
9. Q
10. A

11. C

12. D

13. F

14. I

15. G

16. P

17. K

Definitions List:

Commander-in-Chief - a head of state or officer in supreme command of a country's armed forces

Companions - person or animal with whom one spends a lot of time or with whom one travels

Council - a group of people meeting to talk about important matters and to give advice

Emblem - symbolic object used as an identifying mark

Empire - a major political unit with a large territory or a number of territories or peoples under one ruler with total authority

Founder - one that founds or establishes

Great Spirit - The name that the American Indians gave to God who protected General George Washington

Homage - special honor or respect shown publicly

Leveling - to make or become horizontal, flat, or even

Marksmen - a person skilled in shooting at a mark or target

Mounted British officers - An officer of the British army who patrols on horseback

Particular – very unusual, hard to please

Probability – the likelihood of something happening or being the case

Realization – to be aware of

Seldom – not often

Sharpshooter – one skilled in shooting; a good marksman

Shielding – to cover or screen with or as if with a shield

Chapter 12

Literature Questions

1. A tiny Sunbeam broke through the storm clouds and trickled in through the window like hope broke into his heart.

2. Hope was starting to grow in Mickey's heart that he could believe in God again after his mom's death, and hope was growing Callie's heart to pick a winning photo and believe her dad was okay.

Discussions Questions

1. From God

2. She said yes he does. It's not in words but in a peaceful feeling deep inside.

3. Through the Bible, sermons, prayer, quiet voice of our conscience, sometimes by a something that grabs our attention, like Callie's Neon Light!

4. Know that everyone is separated from God from birth

Know that Jesus died for your sins

Know that Jesus will take away those sins if you ask him to

Jesus will come into your heart and restore a relationship between you and God and give you peace he will become your best friend and never leave you

5. Peaceful – Like a big ole two-ton truck rolled off his chest.

6. Because bitterness and anger can way a person down.

7. Dads listened to what she had learned through the experience. He thought that the good lesson that she had learned was enough.

8. That God has a bigger plan than we can see with our own eyes and it includes others. He wants us to help others and not be selfish

Vocabulary Words - Crossword Puzzle

Word List:

Across:

1. Communication

2. Opportunity

7. Voila

10. Manila-Envelope

11. Impenetrable

Down:

1. Certificate

3. Deserve

4. Khaki

5. Kettle Drum *(a dash is between words to provide a space in the puzzle)*

6. Temptation

8. Sandstorm

9. Separated

Definitions List:

Certificate - a document that is proof of some fact

Communication - an act or instance of transmitting information

Deserve - to be worthy of

Impenetrable - impossible to get through or into

Kettle Drum - a large drum shaped like a bowl, with a membrane adjustable for tension (and so pitch) stretched across.

Khaki - a light yellowish brown color

Manila-Envelope - an envelope designed for transporting documents

Opportunity - a favorable combination of circumstances, time, and place

Sandstorm - a storm of wind (as in a desert) that drives clouds of sand

Separated - to become divided or detached: come apart

Temptation - the state of being tempted especially to evil

Voila - a French exclamation meaning "there it is; there you are"

About the Author

Jan May is author of the New Millennium Girl middle-grade novels for girls: *Isabel's Secret, Isabel's Fun-Fair Fiasco,* and *Callie's Contest of Courage*. She also creates interactive writing books: *Creative Writing Made Easy, Spies of the Revolutionary War Writing Unit,* and *Ocean Adventures in Writing*. During her fifteen years as a creative writing teacher, she has discovered that given the right tools, any child can write—and love it!

New Millennium Girl Books is dedicated to producing wholesome books that inspire vibrant faith. Visit our website for fun homeschool crafts and free writing printables: **www.NewMillenniumGirlBooks.com.**

Isabel Writing Bundle-A Delightful Language Experience! "*Creative Writing Made Easy* with *Isabel's Closet* and *Isabel's Secret* literally rocked our world. I have been struggling to teach my daughter to write. I knew she had the heart of a storyteller, but I could not seem to help her to get all of her stories on paper. Hand her a piece of paper and she would freeze, cry, and fight her way through each assignment. Until we found this series. It transformed writing time from a terror into a delight!" ~Amy Blevins, homeschool mom and owner at Homeschool Copy work

LOOK for our Writing Books for Boys too! Great for the mulit-age classroom!

www.ingramcontent.com/pod-product-compliance
Lightning Source LLC
Chambersburg PA
CBHW060517300426
44112CB00017B/2708